RESTORING A BUS

KENNY BARCLAY

AMBERLEY

Acknowledgements

Although I took well in excess of 1,000 transport photographs during the 1980s and 1990s, strangely I never took any of the vehicles I would go on to preserve. I would therefore like to thank the following people for kindly allowing me to use their photographs within this book. Your help is much appreciated:

Alan Robinson, Andy Higgins JE1791, Andy Lothian T., Adam Conner, Adrian Healey, Alan Urquhart, Barry Sanjana, Barry Young, Campbell Sayers, Chris Platt, Chris Birkett, Christopher Strong, Colin Devine, David Devoy, David Love, Dave Ballantyne, Donald MacRae, George Bobby Black, Gordon Stirling, Iain MacGregor, John Law, John Kennedy, Lindsay Young, Mark Bowerbank, Paul Nicholson, Philip and Sandra Lamb, Phil Halewood, Richard Simons, Rob Newman, Robert McGillivray, Steve Vallance, Steven Booth, Trevor EMDJT42, Vincent Minto, and W. McGregor.

This book is dedicated to my sorely missed grandmother, Christina Barclay, who sadly passed away on Sunday 16 July 2017, just seventy-two days after her 100th birthday. While attending high school, I undertook many trips to Port Glasgow by bus to visit my grandparents after school, and this undoubtedly started my lifelong interest in buses.

First published 2018

Amberley Publishing
The Hill, Stroud
Gloucestershire, GL5 4EP

www.amberley-books.com

Copyright © Kenny Barclay, 2018

The right of Kenny Barclay to be identified as the Author of this work has been asserted in accordance with the Copyrights, Designs and Patents Act 1988.

ISBN 978 1 4456 7372 1 (print)
ISBN 978 1 4456 7373 8 (ebook)

British Library Cataloguing in Publication Data.
A catalogue record for this book is available from the British Library.

Origination by Amberley Publishing.
Printed in the UK.

Contents

Introduction   4

GCS 50V: Alexander AY Leyland Leopard PSU3E/4R   6

HSD 73V: Alexander AD Leyland Fleetline FE30AGR   30

E187 HSF: Alexander RV Volvo Citybus B10M-50/D10M   52

B509 YAT: Plaxton Paramount 3200 Mk 2 Bedford YNT   77

Introduction

Throughout life I have often been asked, 'So why do you like buses?' and I have regularly given thought to this myself. Like most enthusiasts I found myself taking an interest in buses from an early age. In June 1985 Clydeside Scottish Omnibuses was formed and the fleet they inherited from Western Scottish started to receive a wonderful bright red and yellow livery in place of the red and cream Western Scottish livery. I travelled on Clydeside Scottish buses most days, to and from high school and to also visit my grandparents in Port Glasgow most evenings. I started to learn about the vehicles I was traveling on and over time would know if it was a Leyland Leopard or a Seddon Pennine. Being the inquisitive youngster I was, I soon got to know many of the regular drivers, and from talking to them I realised that others shared my interest in buses. I soon joined the Western Enthusiast Club and visited the Scottish Vintage Bus Museum, at that time located in Whitburn. Most of my weekends and holidays would be spent travelling around the west of Scotland, mostly on Clydeside Scottish buses and always taking lots of photographs, but strangely never any photographs of the vehicles I would eventually own. Later, with the help of one of the drivers I got to know well, I was lucky enough to gain a summer job at my local Clydeside Scottish depot at Johnstone. I had a great few weeks learning all about the buses in the fleet and more importantly how to repair and maintain them. This covered everything from re-covering seats, painting and learning how the oily bits worked. Little did I realise that these skills would prove useful later in life, when I eventually owned these same vehicles.

My hobby grew with me over the years and I am now lucky enough to own not one or two, but four preserved vintage buses. I have taken the time to restore each of them back to how they would have looked in the late 1980s, and they all now represent the companies and the years I have the fondest memories of. The first vehicle I purchased was GCS 50V, an Alexander AY-bodied Leyland Leopard from 1980. This was a former Clydeside vehicle and was typical of the type of vehicle that I would regularly travel on in my youth. After much thought and sleepless nights I purchased GCS 50V for the fair price of £1,500 in May 2007. The next three vehicles were purchased over the next two years and represent vehicles that were my favourites back in the day. Although they are all of a similar age, they are all very different: two are double-deck vehicles, two are single-deck vehicles, two have bus seats, one has dual-purpose seating and the other has coach seats, while two are semi-automatic, one is a manual and the other is a full automatic. I have no regrets purchasing any of the vehicles; I know if I had not purchased them when I did then they more than likely would not be around now for others to enjoy. I would not like to add up what I have spent on my buses over the years, but they have ultimately given me great pleasure over the past ten years and will hopefully continue to do so.

If I had to give any one piece of advice to anyone considering restoring a vintage bus, it would be to think carefully about the cost. The initial purchase price is just the start. There are a lot of costs associated with owning a preserved bus including fuel, tyres, insurance, road tax, restoration costs, maintenance costs and finally the ongoing cost of safe secure storage. That said, I would advise anyone that has thought hard about it and has the commitment to definitely go for it. Choose a vehicle that means something to you, restore it at your own pace and to the standard you feel happy with – but most of all, enjoy it!

In this book I look at each of my four vehicles in turn and in the order I purchased them. I start with some information about the type of vehicle along with the vehicle's operating history. I then present a selection of photographs taken of the vehicle throughout its operational working life, showing the many liveries carried. Next, I share some photographs taken on the day I purchased the vehicle, followed by a photographic record of the restoration process. Finally, I have selected some photographs of the completed restored vehicle along with photographs taken at the many open days and events that I have attended with the vehicle. I hope you find this work both interesting and informative.

Kenny Barclay
February 2018

The author, pictured at the wheel of his Leyland Fleetline, HSD 73V.

GCS 50V: Alexander AY Leyland Leopard PSU3E/4R

Vehicle registration number GCS 50V is an Alexander AY-bodied Leyland Leopard PSU3E/4R, which was delivered new to Western SMT in April 1980. After twenty-seven years in passenger service, she was purchased for preservation in May 2007 from West Coast Motors.

Technical Details

Chassis: Leyland Leopard PSU3E/4R
Engine: Leyland 0.680, 11.1 Litre

Bodywork: Alexander AY
Seating Capacity: Fifty-Three Bus Seats

Number: 7903545
Gearbox: Five-Speed Self-Changing Gears
    Pneumocyclic
Number: 138/AY/2078/21
Date First Registered: 10 April 1980.

History

The first Leyland Leopards were constructed in 1959 and were a development of the earlier Leyland Tiger Cub chassis. The chassis were constructed at the Leyland Trucks plant at Farington, Lancashire, with the last examples produced in 1982. At first the Leyland Leopard featured a 9.8-litre 0.600 engine with later examples including GCS 50V receiving the more powerful 11.1-litre 0.680 engine. The Leyland Leopard was hugely successful, with the final examples being withdrawn from public service as late as 2008. The Scottish Bus Group purchased many Leyland Leopards over the years, with Central SMT continuing to opt for a manual gearbox as late as 1979.

The majority of Scottish Bus Group Leyland Leopards received the Alexander Y Type body, and for many years the Alexander Y Type body could be seen the length and breadth of the country. Between 1962 and 1983, over 3,000 Y Type bodies were constructed by Alexanders. The majority, including the bodywork for GCS 50V, were constructed at their Falkirk factory in Scotland, with the remaining bodies being constructed in Belfast. Of the total bodies constructed, two thirds were fitted to Leyland Leopard chassis and over 80 per cent of Y Type vehicles were for Scottish operators.

From 1971 the Y Type technically became known as the AY Type, signifying the bodies were now constructed from alloy, although most people still refer to them as Y Type bodies. There were many variants to the Y Type body; however, the most noticeable difference between the AYS and the AY was the style of windows. The AY body is fitted with long panoramic non-opening windows and the AYS is fitted with narrower windows fitted with opening hoppers. Most Y Type vehicles were fitted with either a wide four-leaf entrance door as fitted to GCS 50V or a narrower two-leaf entrance. Interestingly, emergency exits were fitted to both sides at the rear.

Western SMT purchased a great many Leyland Leopards over the years. GCS 50V represents the final batch of forty vehicles delivered to Western SMT in 1980, and she was first registered on 10 April 1980. She first entered service at Johnstone depot numbered JL50 and would remain at this depot until January 1982, when she was transferred to Western's Dumfries depot. In June 1985 Western Scottish Omnibuses was split, with the northern section of the company becoming Clydeside Scottish Omnibuses. For now, GCS 50V would remain with Western Scottish, and in January 1987 she lost the red and cream livery she had carried from new and received Western's new two-tone grey, black and white livery. She was later renumbered L750.

In August 1989, GCS 50V was transferred south of the border and operated at Carlisle depot before moving back north in November 1989, this time to Greenock depot. In 1989 Clydeside and Western Scottish were merged back together and GCS 50V continued to operate from Greenock depot for approximately six years. This would not be the end of the Clydeside name just yet. Following privatisation of the enlarged Western Scottish, it was agreed that the northern portion, the former Clydeside Scottish area, would be sold to the staff. A new company, Clydeside 2000, commenced trading in October 1991 and quickly introduced a more modern version of the red and yellow Clydeside livery. In November 1991, GCS 50V was the third vehicle to receive the new Clydeside 2000 livery, which she carried until June 1996, whereupon she received Clydeside Buses' red, yellow and white livery. During her six years at Greenock depot she spent just over a year at Inchinnan depot from January 1994 until May 1995. In July 1997 she was withdrawn from front-line service and placed into the reserve fleet.

In August 1997, GCS 50V was sold to Oban & District and quickly gained Oban & District's blue and cream livery while based at Oban depot. In 1999 Oban & District was taken over by West Coast Motors, Campbeltown. Although the Oban & District name continued to be used, the vehicles gradually received the smart red and cream West Coast Motors livery. In August 2006, GCS 50V was on the move again, this time from Oban depot to West Coast Motors Ardrishaig depot. During her time at Ardrishaig depot GCS 50V and sister, ex-Western SMT Leyland Leopard GCS 35V, were predominantly used for school transport work. Following withdrawal from service by West Coast Motors, GCS 50V was purchased for preservation in May 2007, at which point she was just over twenty-seven years old.

Operational Service Photographs

Over the past ten years that I have owned GCS 50V, I have managed to track down many photographs of her operating in passenger service.

GCS 50V is pictured approaching Paisley Cross on her first day in service in April 1980. (David Devoy)

Leyland Leopard DL50 is pictured in Western Scottish livery in the yard at Dumfries Depot. (W. McGregor)

A later view of DL50 in Dumfries town centre, by now wearing Western Scottish black, white and two-tone grey livery. (W. McGregor)

Another view of GCS 50V wearing Western Scottish black, white and two-tone grey livery, this time taken in Kilblain Street, Greenock. GCS 50V moved to Greenock in 1989 and remained in this livery until November 1991. (W. McGregor)

GCS 50V was the third vehicle to be painted into the new Clydeside 2000 livery in November 1991. She is pictured at Church Street, Port Glasgow. (Colin Devine)

GCS 50V is pictured leaving Kilblain Street, Greenock, for Devol in Port Glasgow. She has had her Leyland Leopard badge removed and replaced with a Clydeside 2000 fleet name. (Colin Devine)

A later view of GCS 50V still wearing Clydeside 2000 livery at Kilblain Street, Greenock. Clydeside 2000 initially applied vehicle fleet numbers to all four corners of the vehicle. By this time her fleet number, 750, has been moved from the corners of the vehicle to the centre under the windscreen. (George Bobby Black)

By late 1996, GCS 50V had been repainted into Clydeside Buses' red, yellow and white livery. A final view of GCS 50V during her time in Greenock. The 585 route, which is still operated today by Stagecoach, was a long route that ran from Greenock to Ayr along the Ayrshire coast. (Donald MacRae)

After seventeen years' service in the south-west of Scotland, GCS 50V was sold to Oban & District in August 1997. She is pictured in Oban, wearing her new livery. (Andy Lothian T.)

The blue and cream Oban & District livery suited GCS 50V well. She is pictured at the company's Oban depot. (Donald MacRae)

Following the sale of Oban & District to West Coast Motors, vehicles began to receive West Coast Motors livery. GCS 50V is pictured in Oban during 2002, with the famous McCaig's Tower in the background. (Rob Newman)

Pictured during 2004 at Oban depot, GCS 50V is beginning to look a bit past her best. (Barry Young)

By the time this photograph was taken of GCS 50V departing Oban depot, she had lost her Oban & District fleet names and received West Coast Motors fleet names. (David Devoy)

A final view of GCS 50V during her time with West Coast Motors at Oban. She is pictured at Oban depot in May 2005, surrounded by other former Scottish Bus Group Alexander Y Type Leyland Leopard vehicles that originated in both the Highland Scottish and Fife Scottish fleets. (Phil Halewood)

The Journey to Beith – GCS 50V Begins Her New Life in Preservation

Wednesday 30 May 2007 was the day GCS 50V moved from West Coast Motors depot at Ardrishaig to her new home, the Beith Transport Museum. I did not hold a PSV licence at the time and so fellow enthusiast and friend George kindly offered to be my driver that day. West Coast Motors had two ex-Western Scottish Leyland Leopards at their Ardrishaig depot. Both were due to be withdrawn from service shortly, and so long as I left them with a complete vehicle, I was given permission to swap some seats and various items of interior trim between the two buses. This was much appreciated, since often it's the interior trim and seats that prove the hardest items to track down during restoration. We arrived at Ardrishaig just after 08.00 a.m. and were pleased to see GCS 50V awaiting our attention. Shortly afterwards GCS 35V returned from her school run, and we commenced swapping the various items.

Just after 10.00 a.m., and after a top-up of fuel, it was time for GCS 50V to leave Ardrishaig for the final time. As George was interested in a former Midland Scottish Leyland Leopard that West Coast Motors had for sale at their Oban depot, we decided to travel back to Beith via Oban. After a quick stop at Oban depot, where GCS 50V had spent many years, she passed through the centre of Oban one last time. The journey back to Beith was over 100 miles, and I would be lying if I said I was not apprehensive about how GCS 50V would cope with such a long journey. However, I did not need to worry at all, as she performed very well on what is a very twisty and narrow road with steep hills in places. The only thing that was noted was her reluctance to take second gear. This would definitely need investigation at Beith. We arrived at GCS 50V's new home, the Beith Transport Museum, Ayrshire, just before 17.00 p.m. – a long but satisfying day. It was great to see GCS 50V parked up alongside other preserved vehicles, but I also knew that now the hard work would really begin.

GCS 50V is pictured at West Coast Motors' Ardrishaig depot in the company of fellow former Clydeside Scottish Leyland Leopard GCS 35V. This photograph was taken on the morning I arrived to collect her for preservation.

Right: The interior of GCS 50V was a little tired but not bad for a vehicle that had just completed twenty-seven years' passenger service.

Below: Over the years GCS 50V had received a modified demister system, non-standard driver's seat and modified cab door.

Pictured after arrival at Beith, Ayrshire, GCS 50V still looks smart in her West Coast Motors livery. EFE Models later released a model of GCS 50V wearing this livery.

GCS 50V is pictured parked up inside her new home at the Beith Transport Museum. Her former home depot is still shown on her destination blind.

Restoration

A few days after GCS 50V arrived at the Beith Transport Museum, Stagecoach West Scotland, now owners of the former Western Scottish company, were holding an open day event at their Kilmarnock depot to celebrate their 75th anniversary. Since GCS 50V still had a current MOT certificate, she was therefore able to attend the event. This would be her last trip out before restoration began.

In late July 2007 a full inspection of GCS 50V was undertaken by the mechanics at Beith. The verdict was good; she was in excellent mechanical and electrical condition and the majority of the restoration would involve the interior and exterior. Restoration work began in August 2007, with the biggest mechanical issue being the pneumocyclic gearbox – she was still reluctant to engage second gear. I called West Coast Motors to see if they could shed any light on this issue. What I was not expecting was a kind offer to send a replacement gearbox down to Glasgow that they had in storage. Now that all of their Leyland Leopards had been withdrawn, they no longer required it as a spare. This kind offer was really appreciated and would save me the cost of having the original gearbox repaired. The gearbox arrived a few days later and was quickly fitted to the vehicle, and I was delighted to learn all gears were now working. A full service was then undertaken on GCS 50V, which included changing all oils and filters, adjusting the brakes and greasing all required moving parts. The battery box was found to be in poor condition and a new box was fabricated and fitted. Finally, she was given an underside steam clean and underside paint with protective paint.

Work now turned to the interior. All seat backs and bases were removed before the seat frames were rubbed down and repainted in what can only be described as a dark mustard colour. I was able to match this shade of paint to a section of paint found on the underside of a seat frame. The interior got a heavy clean and the floor was treated to a fresh coat of paint. Although I was able to swap many of the seats and various interior items between GCS 50V and GCS 35V before leaving Ardrishaig, I was still short of a few good-quality seats, and the cab door required replacement as it had been modified over the years. A new cab door was sourced from a local operator that had a former Western Scottish Leopard in long-term storage for parts. Replacement seats came from a source further from home, when I was contacted by an enthusiast in the West Midlands who had a quantity of surplus good-quality seats in the correct moquette for GCS 50V.

Work now turned to the exterior of GCS 50V. I had decided that I wanted GCS 50V to be restored back to the original Clydeside Scottish red and yellow livery as introduced in 1985. Although GCS 50V was a member of the Clydeside fleet, she never actually carried that version of the livery, but did carry the two later versions of the Clydeside livery. During the 1980s and 1990s, buses were mostly hand painted. The paint used would normally be Masons Paints, and I learned of a company in Kilmarnock that was still able to mix paint to the original Masons paint codes if I could find the codes or bring a sample of paint in that it could be matched to. It was at this point I remembered that, many years ago, during my summer employment at the Clydeside Scottish depot in Johnstone, I took a small sample of both the red and yellow paint home and painted a model Routemaster bus. After much hunting around I found the painted model in a storage box and took it back to the paint shop. Success! They quickly matched both shades of paint, which were Signal Red and Lemon Chrome. When Clydeside Scottish first introduced this livery, they fitted most buses with large advertising slogans, 'Welcome Aboard. We're Going Your Way', and 'Hop On' marketing posters and transfers. Again, after some searching in my old storage boxes, I found copies of the original posters and transfers and found a company that could produce replicas. It is an important part of any restoration process to ensure the final result is as accurate as possible.

The next area requiring attention was the exterior of the vehicle. Although she was in good overall condition, many of the body panels had received various dents and damage over the years. The panels are aluminium, so corrosion is not normally an issue. When Alexander's constructed the Y Type vehicles, most vehicles delivered to Western SMT, including GCS 50V, were fitted with larger body panels that folded over and slid up into place on the vertical body supports. This meant that the panels did not require beading strips to be fitted over the edges of the panels, as seen on other Y Type vehicles, with the intention of giving a more modern appearance to the finished vehicle. This style of panel fitment is notoriously difficult to fit, but I was lucky that the coach builder that was changing the panels and completing the exterior of the vehicle had worked with this style of panel before while employed by Western SMT. The restoration of the exterior continued, and along with the replacement of many of the body panels, repairs were also carried out to the fibreglass areas at the front and rear of the vehicle. When new, GCS 50V would have been fitted with a recessed rear number plate behind a glass panel. This was reinstated, along with a 'Pay as you enter' illuminated sign and 'Leyland Leopard' front badge. Many years ago, when attending an open day event at Clydeside Scottish's Greenock depot, I purchased a destination blind. Little did I think at the time that many years later I would have a Clydeside bus that I could fit the blind into.

Once all the body repairs were completed, GCS 50V was repainted by brush into Clydeside Scottish red and yellow livery. New wheel arch trim was ordered from Alexander's and a new black infill strip was fitted to the bodyside trim. This was a difficult and time-consuming task as each section of the strip had to be cut to length and softened in hot water before fitting. The final tasks involved refitting the seats and applying the large advertising slogans, transfers and posters.

On 23 March 2008, the restoration of GCS 50V as Clydeside Scottish G750 was complete.

One of the first tasks needing to be done on GCS 50V was the replacement of a defective gearbox. GCS 50V is seen on the vehicle lifts at Beith, ready for her gearbox to be removed.

The replacement second-hand gearbox is ready to be fitted. Once fitted and tested, an oil and filter change will be carried out.

Once the replacement gearbox was fitted, the underside received a steam clean and paint. The new gearbox can be seen, along with the fluid flywheel, and finally the engine, to the rear of the photograph.

The original battery box was found to be heavily corroded and therefore a new box was fabricated on-site and fitted at Beith.

The front access panels were found to be in poor condition and replacements were fabricated on-site. In this photograph the original demister motors can be seen.

One of the newly fabricated front panels ready to be refitted, complete with the replacement Leyland Leopard badge. GCS 50V carried this badge until her time with Clydeside 2000, when it was removed.

Above: The interior of GCS 50V is stripped and ready for sanding, cleaning and painting.

Right: GCS 50V is beginning to take shape. By this stage her seat frames have been sanded and painted. The floor has also been painted and she is ready for her seats to be refitted.

The replacement front panels have now been refitted, and the body panels that required replacing have been removed. The plastic panel with raised sections below the cab window is fitted to prevent the outer panels vibrating when the vehicle is in traffic.

While the body panels were removed from the vehicle, repairs were also carried out on the frame and fibreglass wheel arches.

By this stage of restoration, the replacement body panels have been started to be fitted. The long cardboard tube contains new wheel arch trim, ordered from Alexander's, which will be cut, shaped and fitted to the vehicle.

Grey undercoat paint has now been applied to the vehicle while fibreglass repairs are carried out around the front of the bus.

The Alexander Y Type design featured a recessed rear number plate fitted behind a glass panel. Over the years this had been removed from GCS 50V, and I was keen to reinstate this feature.

One of the most time-consuming and difficult tasks was the fitting of the many metres of infill strip, which is used to cover the rivets on the bodyside trim.

By the time this photograph was taken on 17 March 2008, the restoration of GCS 50V was almost complete. Painting has just been completed and, once dry, her transfers and advertising slogans will be fitted.

Fleet names and advertising material have now been fitted to the rear of the vehicle. The recessed rear number plate has also been installed by this stage.

The infill strips can be seen to good effect in this photograph. Although fitting the strips was a difficult, time-consuming task, it gives a nice overall finish to the vehicle. The large 'Welcome aboard. We're going your way' advertising slogans have also been fitted.

On 23 March 2008 the restoration of GCS 50V was complete, and Clydeside Scottish vehicle G750 took to the road once more.

The cab has been restored and fitted with a replacement cab door and replacement driver's seat, and has been finished with a Wayfarer ticket machine.

Preservation Life

GCS 50V has settled down into her preserved life. In April 2009 she moved from the Beith Transport Museum to GVVT (Glasgow Vintage Vehicle Trust). Mechanically, she has continued to be a reliable vehicle, requiring only minor running repairs and servicing. One notable exception was in May 2011 during a trip to the Falkirk Wheel when she blew a head gasket. She still made it back to GVVT and was repaired shortly after. Over the years GCS 50V has also required her gear selector to be rewired, brake slack adjusters replaced, brake light switch changed and was also treated to a full set of new tyres. More recently GCS 50V experienced a damaged radiator. Fortunately, I had a replacement in storage, and this was quickly replaced, allowing GCS 50V to return to the road. GCS 50V has attended many events and open days over the years and a selection of photographs taken at these events are shown below.

GCS 50V and HSD 73V are pictured at SVBM in May 2008, taking part in the annual running day event.

Two vintage transportation vehicles pictured together at the Museum of Flight, East Fortune, during a visit in January 2009.

GCS 50V is pictured inside the former Clydeside Scottish Inchinnan depot, taking part in an open day event in August 2009. GCS 50V was allocated to this depot between January 1994 and May 1995.

GCS 50V and HSD 73V are not the only preserved vehicles to carry the Clydeside Scottish livery. Clydeside Scottish operated a large number of former LT Routemaster vehicles and WLT 835 (RM 835) has been preserved in Clydeside Scottish livery. This photograph was taken in October 2010 at the Renfrew Ferry terminal.

Clydeside Buses became part of the Arriva Group. In March 2011, to help celebrate the launch of a new book covering the history of Clydeside Scottish, written by its former Managing Director, Arriva vehicle P801 RWU was repainted into Clydeside Scottish livery. The extremely smart pair of vehicles are pictured in the yard at Johnstone depot.

In September 2011, an event was held at coachbuilders Alexander's Falkirk factory to celebrate fifty years of the Y Type design. A large number of Y Type vehicles, including the first and last built, took part in the event.

HSD 73V: Alexander AD Leyland Fleetline FE30AGR

Vehicle registration number HSD 73V is an Alexander AD-bodied Leyland Fleetline FE30AGR, which was delivered new to Western SMT in July 1980. She remained in passenger service until May 2005, before being preserved. She later passed to me for continued preservation in November 2007.

Technical Details

Chassis: Leyland Fleetline FE30AGR
Engine: Gardner 6LXB, 10.45 Litre
Bodywork: Alexander AD
Seating Capacity: Seventy-Five (44/31) Bus Seats

Number: 7905633
Gearbox: Four-Speed Daimatic Epicyclic
Number: AD19/779/4
Date First Registered: 2 July 1980

History

The earlier Fleetline chassis were constructed by Daimler of Coventry, with the first example being unveiled at the 1960 Earls Court Motor show. The rear-engined Fleetline chassis was Daimler's answer to the Leyland Atlantean, which was also a rear-engined chassis that rival manufacturer Leyland had launched in 1958.

Both vehicles featured a similar layout, with the engine transversely mounted at the rear of the vehicle. However, on the Daimler Fleetline the gearbox, a Daimatic four-speed, was mounted separately from the engine. This was intended to help reduce the build-up of heat. The other most noticeable difference with the Daimler Fleetline was the drop centre rear axle. This ensured that the lower-deck floor could be flat, which then permitted normal seating on both decks on what was a low-height vehicle. Initially, the Fleetline was supplied with the 102 hp Gardner 6LW engine. This was later changed to the more powerful 150 hp 6LX engine, with later models including HSD 73V receiving the 180 hp 6LXB engine. From 1970 the Leyland o.680 engine was also an option.

The Fleetline remained in production until 1981, by which time over 11,700 chassis had been constructed. Construction at Coventry continued until 1973 before moving to the Leyland plant at Farington, Lancashire. In 1975 the Fleetline chassis designations were changed to Leyland codes and the Fleetline was then sold as the Leyland Fleetline.

The Alexander AD Type body ('A' signifying a later body featuring alloy construction) first appeared in 1963 and was a low-height version of the earlier Alexander A or J Type body. Over 550 D Type bodies were constructed by Alexander's, mostly being fitted to Fleetline chassis before the type was replaced by the R Type in 1981.

Western SMT purchased over 250 Fleetlines between 1960 and 1980. Most were fitted with Alexander bodywork, but many also received Northern Counties bodies. HSD 73V represents the final batch of twenty Alexander-bodied Fleetlines delivered to Western SMT in 1980 and she was first registered on 2 July 1980. She would enter service shortly after at Dumfries depot numbered DR73, and would remain at this depot until May 1982, when she was transferred north to Western's Thornliebank depot. When delivered she was fully automatic, but during her time with Clydeside Scottish she was converted to semi-automatic. In June 1985 Western Scottish Omnibuses was split, with the northern section of the company becoming Clydeside Scottish Omnibuses. HSD 73V, now numbered M73, received Clydeside's new bright red and yellow livery in 1986. In 1989 Clydeside and Western Scottish were merged back together and HSD 73V continued to operate from Thornliebank depot, now numbered MR973.

Following privatisation of the enlarged Western Scottish, it was agreed that the northern portion, the former Clydeside Scottish area, would be sold to the staff. A new company, Clydeside 2000, commenced trading in October 1991, and quickly introduced a more modern version of the red and yellow Clydeside livery. HSD 73V passed to the new Clydeside 2000 company, and although she would receive Clydeside 2000 fleet names, she never received the new Clydeside 2000 livery despite other Fleetlines being repainted at this time. During her time with Clydeside 2000, she remained allocated predominantly to Thornliebank depot, but also spent some time in the early 1990s allocated to both Inchinnan and Johnstone depots. She received fleet number 873, and at times this was preceded with depot code M for Thornliebank. Thornliebank depot replaced Newton Mearns depot, but the M depot code was retained for Thornliebank depot. Around May 1994 she was re-registered with a former London Transport Routemaster registration, becoming 705 DYE. This did not last long, as the Routemaster registration was transferred to a coach a few months later. At this time she received registration number WDS 112V, which she carried until entering into preservation.

In May 1996, WDS 112V, now allocated to Johnstone depot, was withdrawn from service and subsequently sold to North (dealer) in Sherburn-in-Elmet, East Yorkshire.

She was then purchased for further service by TM Travel, Staveley, Derbyshire and remained with TM Travel until March 2002, at which point she passed to Tim Draper Travel, Tibshelf, Alfreton. She would remain in service with Tim Draper until May 2005 before being purchased for preservation, by which time she had completed twenty-five years in passenger service.

Operational Service Photographs

Over the past ten years that I have owned HSD 73V, I have managed to track down many photographs of her operating in passenger service.

Pictured not long after entering service, HSD 73V is seen wearing Western Scottish red and cream livery at Dumfries Sandgate. (Lindsay Young)

HSD 73V is pictured heading along Argyle Street, Glasgow, pursued by a Glasgow PTE Leyland Atlantean. This photograph would have been taken after May 1982, by which time HSD 73V was allocated to Thornliebank depot. (David Devoy)

Pictured while parked up at Glasgow Anderston bus station, MR73 awaits departure back to Neilston, Renfrewshire. (Alan Urquhart)

By the time this photograph was taken in late 1986, the Glasgow bus scene had changed dramatically. HSD 73 V, now resplendent in Clydeside red and yellow livery, is pictured heading down Union Street in the company of Strathclyde Buses and Kelvin Scottish vehicles. (Gordon Stirling)

HSD 73 V is pictured at Hill Drive, Eaglesham, by which time she has been fitted with large 'Hop On' logos at either side of her destination display. (Steven Booth)

After Western and Clydeside Scottish were merged back together in 1989, HSD 73V was renumbered from M73 to MR973. She is pictured heading south on Eglinton Street, Glasgow. (Philip Lamb)

Now part of the Clydeside 2000 fleet and carrying fleet number M873, HSD 73V is pictured on Renfrew Road, approaching Paisley. (W. McGregor)

This photograph was taken around May 1994 at Johnstone depot. She now carries fleet number 873 and has now received registration number 705 DYE from former LT Routemaster RM1705, which Clydeside Scottish acquired in 1987 for spare parts. (Adam Conner)

When this photograph of 873 was taken at Glasgow Buchanan bus station, she had been re-registered again. She now carries registration WDS 112V, which she continued to carry until shortly after she was preserved. She now carries Clydeside 2000 fleet names but never received the new Clydeside 2000 livery, as seen on HSD 77V, which is parked next to her in this photograph. (Steve Vallance)

WDS 112V is pictured passing through Paisley Cross in September 1995. This photograph was taken less than a year before she would be withdrawn from service and sold to a dealer in East Yorkshire. (George Bobby Black)

By October 1996, WDS 112V had been purchased by TM Travel, Staveley. She is pictured at the company's depot, having been freshly repainted into TM Travel livery. Note that she has also been fitted with a cast Daimler badge on her front panel. (Adrian Healey)

This photograph of WDS 112V was taken at Chesterfield station in April 2001, less than a year before she would be withdrawn by TM Travel. By this time her lower front panel has been painted red, which suits the rest of the livery much better. She has also lost her Daimler badge. (Trevor EMDJT42)

Following withdrawal by TM Travel, WDS 112V passed to Tim Draper Travel, Alfreton. She remained in service with Tim Draper until May 2005 and is pictured at Mortimer Wilson School, Alfreton, in January 2003. (Adrian Healey)

Preservation: The First Few Years

HSD 73V first entered preservation on 2 May 2005 when she was purchased by two members of the GVVT from Tim Draper and brought back to Scotland. At the time she carried registration number WDS 112V, but on 29 May 2006 she was re-registered back to her original number, HSD 73V. Restoration progressed over the next eighteen months, but in November 2007 the current owner decided to sell her to me so that he could focus on his other preservation projects.

On 28 November 2007, HSD 73V was moved from GVVT to the Beith Transport Museum, where my Leyland Leopard was already located and being restored. The journey to Beith was made via Glasgow, Paisley and Johnstone – all locations that HSD 73V would have visited regularly over the years in service with Clydeside Scottish. Upon arrival at Beith it was wonderful to have these two former Clydeside vehicles together, and I looked forward to seeing them both completely restored and wearing Clydeside Scottish livery.

WDS 112V, with her destination blind correctly set, is pictured in May 2005 while getting ready to depart Alfreton for her new preserved life in Glasgow. (John Kennedy)

The interior of the lower-deck, while in reasonable condition for her age, had many of the seats covered in wrong moquette and will require to be re-covered. (John Kennedy)

By 2007, WDS 112V had regained her original registration number, HSD 73V. She is pictured getting ready to depart from GVVT, for her new home at the Beith Transport Museum following purchase by the author.

The upper-deck interior had been partially stripped and restored; however, much more work was still needed to be completed.

Restoration

A three-month push to complete the restoration of HSD 73V was started in February 2008, just as the restoration of my Clydeside Scottish Leyland Leopard GCS 50V was nearing completion. The restoration process included extensive body repairs, re-panel work and finally a repaint into the original Clydeside Scottish livery of red and yellow, which she carried during the late 1980s.

Most of the bodywork appeared to be in fairly good condition. Following an inspection by the team at Beith it was decided that many of the lower panels would require changing, along with minor fibreglass repairs needing doing around the front. The body panels fitted to HSD 73V were again aluminium panels. Although aluminium is expensive, the damaged panels being removed were able to go for scrap, which helped reduce the overall cost. Watching the lower panels being replaced on my Fleetline reminded me of my time working at Johnstone depot many years before. I recall being shown how to change a body panel by first drilling out the rivets holding the panel and beading strips in place. The damaged panel can then be removed and used as a template for cutting and folding a new panel. I remember that Johnstone depot painted one side of the panels red and the other yellow. This would ensure that, if it was cut and folded the correct way, it would be ready painted once fitted to the vehicle. When some of the panels were removed between the upper- and lower-decks, it revealed the body number in marker pen on the body frame. Next to the number was the word 'Western', which presumably was to remind the coachbuilders at Alexander's that this vehicle was destined for Western SMT. The Fleetline vehicle is rear-engined, and therefore features a large, heavy, fibreglass cowling and lid covering the engine, radiator and gearbox. This again required a bit of fibreglass repair work and a replacement metal grill to replace the heavily corroded radiator cover. After much trial and error, we found we could not get the engine cover lid to sit properly. Eventually, I decided to change the cover with a spare one I had inherited with the vehicle. This fitted much better, and following painting, the rear of the vehicle started to take shape. Over the next few weeks the vehicle received a red and yellow undercoat, followed by a red and yellow top coat of the same paint used earlier on my Leyland Leopard.

To complete the exterior of the vehicle, large 'Welcome aboard. We're going your way' slogans were applied. Although they were the same as the slogans fitted to my Clydeside Leyland Leopard, these slogans were yellow rather than red. I also decided to fit large 'Hop On' logos on either side of the destination box at the front of the vehicle. Hop On was a 1980s post-deregulation Scottish Bus Group marketing campaign. Clydeside, Central and Kelvin Scottish all participated, selling and accepting the Hop On multi-journey tickets. Most vehicles, including HSD 73V, which operated for the three Scottish Bus Group companies in the Strathclyde area carried these logos. Applying all the transfers, legal lettering, stickers and posters is a stage of the restoration process I always find very satisfying; tracking down old photographs of the vehicle taken wearing the livery, watching them being recreated and ensuring everything is positioned correctly is very rewarding.

The interior of the vehicle also needed a bit of work. First, all upper-deck seat frames were removed, sanded and repainted. While the seat frames were removed, some damaged Formica wall panels were replaced. The previous owner had already managed to track down some replacement plastic trim for the upper-deck front windowsill. This had involved a trip to a scrapyard in Yorkshire, where a sister vehicle from the same batch was being dismantled for scrap. As already pointed out, it's the small items of interior trim that can prove the hardest to track down, but if they can be found it makes all the difference to the restoration. When restoring a vehicle, if a similar donor vehicle can be purchased and stripped as a source of spare parts, it will be well worth it in the long term. The interior received a deep clean, roof to floor, before the seat frames were refitted. A few of the seats required replacing and this was undertaken by myself using some spare moquette, a sewing machine and a staple gun. Hop On marketing stickers were fitted inside the vehicle. These had been carefully reproduced from an original that had been safely stored for many years.

Mechanically, HSD 73V was in great shape. A full service was carried out, including all oils, filters and lubricants. The Gardner engine was found to be in good condition and all filters are still able to be obtained fairly easily. Over the years HSD 73V had been fitted with a tachograph rather than a conventional speedometer. The tachograph had been fitted up near the windscreen and I decided that I would prefer to reinstate the conventional speedometer in place of the tachograph. This involved a fair bit of wiring work, which was carried out at a local haulier's premises that specialised in tachographs. Finally, prior to MOT testing it was discovered that HSD 73V required replacement brake shoes and slack adjusters fitted to the front nearside wheel. Once this work was undertaken she was presented for MOT and passed with no issues noted.

Restoration was finally completed on 14 May 2008 and I was delighted to see HSD 73V and GCS 50V side by side in Clydeside Scottish livery.

The missing black plastic trim required to complete the restoration of the top-deck front window is pictured getting fitted. The parts required were obtained from a sister vehicle being broken for spares by a Yorkshire vehicle dismantler. (John Kennedy)

When this photograph was taken, the majority of the upper-deck seats had been removed to permit them to be sanded and painted. At the same time some damaged Formica panels were replaced. (John Kennedy)

With an upper side panel now removed, the construction of the top-deck floor can be seen. The lower curved section forms the lower-deck roof and the upper curved section forms the upper-deck floor.

With some of the lower panels now removed, the frame of HSD 73V can be repaired where needed. The white plastic panels with the raised sections are fitted throughout the vehicle between the outer and inner panels to stop the aluminium body panels vibrating and becoming damaged.

HSD 73V had completed twenty-five years in passenger service. Once the lower panels were removed, some damage to the rear wheel arches and frame was revealed. This was repaired before the new body panels were fitted.

By the time this photograph was taken in April 2008, the lower-frame repairs had been completed and she was ready to have her new body panels fitted.

Just twelve days after the last photograph was taken, HSD 73V had her new lower-deck panels and beading strips fitted.

While the lower-deck area of HSD 73V receives restoration work to her body panels, the painter has made a start to the upper-deck and roof.

Right: The metal radiator grill was found to be heavily corroded, and a spare in good condition was sourced. In this photograph the new grill has been fitted and is awaiting painting.

Below: When this photograph was taken in May 2008, much of the rear engine cover has been repaired and painted. Unfortunately, the engine cover lid fitted to HSD 73V was damaged and would not sit correctly.

A replacement engine cover lid for HSD 73V was provided with the vehicle by the previous owner, and in this view is having some minor repairs carried out before being fitting to the vehicle.

With the replacement engine cover lid now fitted to HSD 73V, and the rear end painted in a pink undercoat, M73 is beginning to take shape.

Right: By 13 May 2008, painting of the roof, upper-deck and wheels was complete. The rest of the vehicle was in an undercoat, awaiting application of the top coat.

Below: With all fibreglass repairs now complete and just the lower-deck panels to be painted, the restoration of HSD 73V is almost complete.

HSD 73V is pictured outside the Beith Transport Museum in the spring sunshine. Her restoration is now virtually complete and she awaits the fitting of her fleet names and advertising slogans.

The completed upper-deck of M73. All seat frames have been sanded and repainted, the front and rear roof domes have been repainted and any damaged seats have been re-covered in the correct moquette. She has also received a detailed heavy clean throughout.

HSD 73V is pictured outside the Beith Transport Museum on 14 May 2008 following the completion of her restoration. She has been fitted with large 'Hop On' logos and 'Welcome aboard. We're going your way' advertising slogans, which she would have carried during her time with Clydeside Scottish.

Preservation Life, After Restoration

Since her restoration was completed in 2008, HSD 73V has settled down and been a reliable vehicle. In April 2009 she moved along with my Clydeside Leyland Leopard GCS 50V from the Beith Transport Museum back to GVVT (Glasgow Vintage Vehicle Trust). Over the past few years she has required the remaining brake shoes and liners to be replaced. She has also required some minor wiring work to her cab light, engine stop solenoid, speedo drive and horn. During the past two winters I have spent time removing years of rust from the chassis and coating the chassis in anti-corrosive paint. HSD 73V has attended many events and open days over the years and a selection of photographs taken at these events are shown below.

My two Clydeside Scottish vehicles, GCS 50V and HSD 73V, are pictured outside the Beith Transport Museum shortly before departing to attend an open day event at SVBM.

GCS 50V and HSD 73V take pride of place at Arriva's Inchinnan depot during an open day event in August 2009, held to celebrate a fleet of new vehicles entering into service. At times both vehicles had operated from Inchinnan depot when part of the Clydeside Scottish fleet.

In October 2011 I was asked by a good friend if we could take HSD 73V for a day trip out to the island of Rothesay. I must admit to being rather nervous about taking HSD 73V on a ferry. However, I need not have worried, as HSD 73V performed very well that day.

While on the island of Rothesay we called into the West Coast Motors depot. This was a former Clydeside Scottish depot in 1985, and prior to that was a tram depot on the island. It is believed this was the first time HSD 73V had visited this depot, and indeed the island of Rothesay.

Clydeside Scottish M73 is pictured in the afternoon sun in November 2011 at Bishopton, Renfrewshire.

On 4 July 2012, HSD 73V and a selection of other vintage vehicles from the GVVT collection attended an event at George Square, Glasgow, to mark the diamond jubilee of Queen Elizabeth II. The upper-deck of HSD 73V provided an excellent viewing platform to watch the Queen taking part at this prestigious event.

On 15 July 2017, M73 took part in a running day event organised by Glasgow City Council, linking many of the museums of Glasgow. It was a most enjoyable day, with HSD 73V being a popular choice for many visitors. She is pictured heading up Queen Street, Glasgow, past Royal Exchange Square. (Paul Nicholson)

E187 HSF: Alexander RV Volvo Citybus B10M-50/D10M

Vehicle registration number E187 HSF is an Alexander RV-bodied Volvo Citybus B10M-50/ D10M, which was one of four delivered new to Eastern Scottish in August 1987. She entered service with Eastern Scottish at Dalkeith depot and remained at this depot for the majority of her working life. Eastern Scottish later became Eastern SMT before becoming part of First Group. She remained in passenger service until February 2008 before being purchased from First Group for preservation, at the time still allocated to Dalkeith Depot.

Technical Details

Chassis: Volvo Citybus B10M-50/D10M
Engine: Volvo TDH100, 9.60 Litre

Bodywork: Alexander RV
Seating Capacity: Eighty (45/35) Dual-Purpose Seats

Number: YV31MGB12HA014982
Gearbox: Four-Speed Voith D854.2 Automatic
Number: 25/2386/1
Date First Registered: 14 August 1987

History

The Volvo Citybus was the first successful commercially produced underfloor-engined double-decker bus in the UK. The first example, which was fitted with an eighty-six-seat Marshall body, entered service in Glasgow with Strathclyde PTE in 1982. The Citybus followed on from the front-engined Volvo Ailsa and was based on the highly successful mid-engined B10M coach chassis. Until this time double-deck buses would have the engine located either at the front or rear of the vehicle. As vehicle designs changed over the years to become more suitable for OMO (one-man operation), more and more manufactures moved the engine from the front to the rear of the vehicle. A notable exception was the Volvo Ailsa, introduced in 1974, which featured an engine at the front next to the driver. This location of the engine made the vehicle noisy for the driver and often resulted in an awkward entrance and staircase layout. The Ailsa was never a big seller compared to other vehicles at the time and Volvo was therefore keen to replace the Ailsa with a double-deck vehicle based on one of its existing chassis, choosing the B10M. With the Citybus being based on both the Volvo Ailsa and the Volvo B10M chassis, it featured air bag suspension, a 9.6-litre Volvo THD100 engine and a perimeter chassis frame. One of the most attractive features of the Volvo Citybus was the seating capacity. Having the engine mounted under the floor meant that the seating capacity could be as high as eighty-six compared to many rear-engined double-deck vehicles that seated just seventy-five. One downside of the Citybus was, however, the height of the floor. Having the engine mounted under the floor mid-vehicle meant the floor was higher than rear-engined vehicles. This was often compensated by fitting Citybus vehicles, including E187 HSF, with low-profile tyres. The Citybus was offered with a choice of three gearboxes: SCG (Self-Changing Gears), Voith or ZF. The Voith and ZF gearboxes featured an integral retarder and were the most popular gearboxes fitted of the three offered.

E187 HSF was delivered with a five-speed ZF gearbox, but over the years this was changed to a three-speed Voith D851.2 gearbox. In her preserved life she has now been fitted with a four-speed Voith D854.2 gearbox.

The first Citybus vehicles delivered were fitted with Marshall's bodywork, quickly followed by East Lancs and Northern Counties. It would be 1984 before any Citybus vehicles were delivered with Alexander's bodywork, with the first examples being delivered to Strathclyde PTE. Alexanders would eventually go on to provide the bodywork for just over half of all Volvo Citybus vehicles constructed. The original design of the Alexander R Type body fitted to earlier Volvo Citybus vehicles featured a large radiator grill, similar to that fitted to the Volvo Ailsa vehicles. This was changed in around 1987 to a revised design, which featured a less prominent radiator grill, but was still very different to the R Type lower-front panel fitted to Leyland and MCW vehicles.

The first two Alexander-bodied Volvo Citybus vehicles delivered to the Scottish Bus Group were two vehicles delivered to Fife Scottish in 1984 with a stylish coach-type bodywork, known as the RVC body, which was based on the Alexander TC coach. In 1986 Leyland also introduced an underfloor-engined double-deck bus known as the Leyland Lion. The vehicle was fitted with a Leyland TL11 engine and remained in production for just two years, with a total of only thirty-two Leyland Lions being constructed. The Volvo Citybus fared much better, with a total of 575 vehicles being delivered between 1982 and 1993. The biggest customer by far was Strathclyde PTE, who purchased a total of 101, most being delivered between 1989 and 1990.

With the Volvo Citybus being based on the Volvo B10M coach chassis, the Citybus vehicles were very powerful and comfortable vehicles. They could easily keep up with most coaches on the road at the time and operators often specified them with either dual-purpose or coach-style seating, as fitted to E187 HSF. The Citybus was often ordered as a vehicle intended to provide comfortable inter-urban express services and was often used by companies to introduce a more attractive service to help win passengers in the recently deregulated marketplace.

E187 HSF was one of four Volvo Citybus vehicles delivered to Eastern Scottish in 1987 and these were the last Citybus vehicles delivered to Eastern Scottish. She was fitted with the revised style of the Alexander RV bodywork with eighty dual-purpose seats. She entered service in August 1987 as ZVV187 at Dalkeith depot, and, with the exception of a couple of brief transfers to Livingston and North Berwick depots, she would spend the next twenty-one years at Dalkeith, operating services to and from Edinburgh city centre.

She has carried a number of liveries over the years. The first livery she carried from new was a two-tone green and cream livery, similar to the livery carried by an earlier batch of Alexander RH-bodied Leyland Lions from 1986. This is the livery that I chose to restore E187 HSF back to as I feel it was the most attractive livery she had carried over the years. By 1989, E187 HSF, along with the other Volvo Citybus vehicles in this batch, received a modified version of the two-tone green and cream livery, featuring a much larger area of dark green on her lower panels. This was maybe intended to hide some of the road grime that could often be seen on the earlier version of the livery. Strangely, the panel around her headlamps remained painted in cream, which gave a rather odd look to the front of the vehicle. She now carried the fleet number VV187, and in September 1990 Eastern Scottish was privatised and sold to the employees. It became known as SMT and over time the Eastern Scottish fleet names were changed to SMT with a diamond logo. This version of the livery did not last long as by 1993 she had regained the original version of the livery, with cream lower panels and just a small dark green skirt. In October 1994, SMT was purchased by the GRT Group, and shortly after the company became known as First SMT. At this time, E187 HSF received a mostly cream with two-tone green livery applied in GRT Group style and carried SMT Lothians fleet names. She was also renumbered, becoming 2187 in the new company. In 1997, First SMT was merged with Midland Bluebird and Lowland to become First Edinburgh. With the formation of the new larger merged company, a new livery was introduced. E187 HSF was soon renumbered as 1187 and was repainted into the new livery of darker cream with a green, yellow and a blue band. The three colours represented the colours of the three companies that had been merged to become First Edinburgh. She would receive one final livery during her time with First Edinburgh, and by 2003 she had received First Group corporate white, pink and blue livery. There were two versions of this livery. The version with the white and blue swoop on the side was intended to be applied to new vehicles only and became known as 'Barbie' livery. The other version of the livery, known as 'Barbie 2', was applied to older vehicles that First had inherited. It was this version of the livery that was applied to E187 HSF and it featured a faded-out pink band between the white and blue sections of the livery. Interestingly, other members of the same batch of four vehicles as E187 HSF received the full 'Barbie' livery, which was intended for new vehicles only. During her time with First Group she later received national fleet number 31632.

Over the years she has almost always been allocated to Dalkeith depot. However, during 1994 she spent a short period of time at Livingston depot, and in 1997 she spent a period of time allocated to North Berwick depot. When I purchased her for preservation in February 2008 from First Group she was still allocated to Dalkeith depot. At that time, she was the last of the four Citybuses delivered to Eastern Scottish in 1987 still in service, and was most probably the last Eastern Scottish vehicle to be found still in passenger service.

Operational Service Photographs

Over the past ten years that I have owned E187 HSF I have managed to track down many photographs of her operating in passenger service, including photographs of her in each of the liveries she has carried.

E187 HSF is pictured departing from St Andrews bus station, Edinburgh, in October 1987, just two months after entering service. Of the six liveries she carried while in public service, this photograph represents the livery I have chosen for her restoration. (Vincent Minto)

Pictured heading east along Edinburgh's Princes Street on her way to Polton Mill, this photograph of VV187 G captures the dual-purpose seating fitted to this vehicle. When I purchased her for preservation over twenty years later, she was still fitted with these seats. (Gordon Stirling)

By 1989, E187 HSF had received a revised version of her Eastern Scottish livery, featuring a much larger area of dark green on her lower panels. This was perhaps intended to hide some of the road grime that could often be seen on the earlier version of the livery. (John Law)

VV187 G is pictured heading to Rosewell, hotly pursued by a Lothian Regional Transport Leyland Atlantean. With the revised version of the livery, I always felt the cream panel around the headlamps looked odd. (W. McGregor)

By 1993, E187 HSF had been repainted back to the original version of the Eastern Scottish livery, albeit with SMT fleet names and logos in place of her Eastern Scottish fleet names. (Campbell Sayers)

E187 HSF is pictured in SMT livery at St Andrews bus station, Edinburgh, getting ready to depart to Bathgate. This photograph was taken in 1995, during the period of time she was allocated to Livingston depot. (Robert McGillivary)

VV187 N is pictured departing Buchanan bus station, Glasgow, in May 1995 while operating Diamond service X34 to Livingston. (Barry Sanjana)

This 1997 view of E187 HSF, by now renumbered 2187, was taken at Leith Docks while operating a private hire. She now carries the GRT (Grampian Regional Transport) style of the SMT livery. (David Love)

It was not long before E187 HSF was repainted in yet another livery; this time it was the new First Edinburgh livery. This livery featured a darker cream colour with three coloured bands, which represented the colours of the three companies (Eastern, Lowland and Midland) that had been merged to form First Edinburgh. (Andy Higgins JE1791)

E187 HSF is pictured in First Edinburgh livery, heading west along Edinburgh's Princes Street in June 2002. By this time she had lost her front fog lamps. (Christopher Strong)

A charming evening view of E187 HSF awaiting departure to Birkenside taken in February 2003. When this photograph was taken, the Dennis Dart vehicle behind carried First Group 'Barbie' livery, and it would not be long before E187 HSF also received the new First corporate livery. (Christopher Strong)

This photograph of E187 HSF heading along Edinburgh's Princes Street was taken shortly after she was repainted into First Group's new corporate livery. (Chris Birkett)

E187 HSF is pictured heading west along Edinburgh's Princes Street in May 2003. This version of the First Group corporate livery was known as 'Barbie 2' and was intended for vehicles that First had inherited, with 'Barbie' livery being retained for new vehicles. (Mark Bowerbank)

When this photograph of E187 HSF was taken in October 2006, she had clocked up nineteen years in passenger service and, interestingly, she still retained her original dual-purpose seats. By this time she had also received her new First Group national fleet number, 31632. (Robert McGillivary)

Taken during her final year of passenger service in July 2007, E187 HSF is pictured at North Bridge, Edinburgh. By this time her lower 'via' destination screen had been blanked over. Pleasingly, when I removed the painted-out section I discovered the original 'via' blind was still in place. (Dave Ballantyne)

E187 HSF Leaves Corporate Life for Preservation

I initially contacted First Group in December 2007 to enquire if E187 HSF would be available to purchase for preservation. First Group's policy at the time dictated that vehicles withdrawn from service would only be sold for scrap or occasionally for preservation. If sold for preservation, it was stipulated that the vehicle was not permitted to be resold back to an operator for commercial use.

Within a short period of time, I was informed that my request to purchase E187 HSF for preservation had been approved and that I would be contacted when she became available. I kept in regular contact with the First Edinburgh fleet engineer and the depot manager at Dalkeith depot, and at the beginning of February 2008 I was informed the vehicle had now been withdrawn from service. Before purchasing the vehicle, I arranged to visit the depot at Dalkeith and have a look over E187 HSF. I was pleased with what I found and felt that the vehicle was, overall, in good condition for her age. She still retained her original seats and the interior was in a good original condition, including her lower-rear window, which had not been removed and plated over. The vehicle was purchased from First Group on 22 February 2008 and I arranged to collect the vehicle from Dalkeith depot a few days later on 25 February 2008.

When purchasing a vehicle for preservation from a bus operator, the tyres often have to be purchased at an extra cost. This is because the tyres fitted to the bus are often on a contract with one of the larger tyre manufactures and are therefore not owned by the bus company. A price to purchase the tyres outright can be obtained from the tyre company, but it is often cheaper to source your own tyres. I was able to source my own tyres from a local Ayrshire company at a keen price and First Group kindly let me collect E187 HSF with their tyres still on the vehicle, so long as they were returned the following week.

The journey from Dalkeith back to the Beith Transport Museum went without a hitch and within a few days E187 HSF was fitted with her new tyres. I returned the tyres to First the following week and at the same time I arranged to visit First's Livingston depot, where two sister vehicles to E187 HSF, E189 HSF and E190 HSF, were located and withdrawn, awaiting scrapping. These two vehicles had recently had their seats reupholstered in the original moquette and proved to be a fantastic source of spare parts, including replacement seats, an original Eastern Scottish-style cab door and various bits of trim.

E187 HSF is pictured on 25 February 2008 inside Dalkeith depot, *definitely* awaiting my collection. I am not, however, convinced that this was the managing director's vehicle.

This photograph of the cab area shows how years of service have taken their toll on E187 HSF. At some point she has received an incorrect cab seat, has lost a handrail and her Eastern Scottish-style cab door has been removed.

Although the majority of her seats were of a dual-purpose style in the original moquette, many were in poor condition, and many still had ashtrays fitted, showing their age.

Restoration

E187 HSF was in a good overall condition when I purchased her. I decided I would keep her on the road for the remainder of 2008, and during this time she attended a few events and open days as First 31632.

Her restoration began in December 2008 and was completed in March 2009. Mechanically, it was found that she was in good condition. Unfortunately, most of her body panels had suffered damage over the years and many more had to be replaced due to the fitting of advert frames that, when removed, would leave holes in the bodywork. Overall, approximately 70 per cent of the aluminium body panels had to be replaced.

As mentioned earlier, E187 HSF had received 'Barbie 2' livery. This version of the First Group livery featured a faded-out pink section of the livery that was applied between the white and blue sections. This faded-out pink section was actually a sticky vinyl film and would prove very difficult and time-consuming to remove. While I spent many hours with a heat gun, scraper and cans of Nitromors, trying to remove all traces of pink, the coachbuilder at Beith began to change the damaged panels. The panels that did not require changing were sanded and repaired. As they were sanded, the various earlier liveries were uncovered.

When I purchased E187 HSF from First Group, I noticed that the front fog lamps had been plated over. When I looked in behind the front bumper, I noticed that the original fog lamps were still in place. I then removed the metal plates and checked the fog lamps for any damage. They were both in excellent condition but unfortunately did not work. After a little investigation by the resident electrician we were able to get the lights working.

By this stage all the panels requiring replacing had been replaced and the vehicle had been sanded and prepared for painting. I had decided that I would restore her to her original Eastern Scottish two-tone green and cream livery with large Eastern Scottish logos. An all-over grey undercoat was applied first before the cream and green sections were added. I had assumed that the painter would paint the vehicle in the cream livery with dark green skirt and roof and then add in the light green 'flashes' on the sides. The painter, however, decided to show off his skills by painting the light green sections first and filling in the cream sections after. Slowly, the finished vehicle took shape. The painter confessed it was one of the more difficult liveries he had been asked to recreate, but agreed that the vehicle looked fantastic once complete.

While the exterior was being transformed, I turned my attention to the interior. All the seats were still in the original moquette, but many had seen better days. I set about replacing the seats that were in the worst condition with the seats I had salvaged from the sister vehicles awaiting scrap at Livingston. This gave me a full set of good-condition seats with a few spares if needed. I also replaced the cab door with the Eastern Scottish-style door I had earlier sourced and removed the bright green paint that had been applied to all the handrails and poles. The destination screen fitted to E187 HSF was a modern large display with both an ultimate destination and a 'via' blind. The glass covering the original 'via' blind had been painted out, but, pleasingly, the blind was still in place. I managed to track down a replacement period ultimate destination blind and it was soon fitted in E187 HSF.

Next, I repainted the wheels in cream with a green centre and fitted a set of shiny new silver wheel nut rings to the front wheels. Before E187 HSF took to the road I fitted the large Eastern Scottish fleet names on her side panels with a smaller Eastern Scottish fleet name front and rear. Unfortunately, this took two attempts as the first 'large' fleet names I ordered were not large enough! The final touches included fitting her original fleet number, VV187, along with a new Alexander's badge and Volvo badge front and rear.

Restoration was finally completed on 29 March 2009, and I was delighted to see E187 HSF sitting alongside my other two restored vehicles, HSD 73V and GCS 50V.

E187 HSF is pictured in December 2008 as her restoration begins. The first few body panels have been removed, which revealed some corrosion around the wheel arch areas and lower-back end.

The lower panels around the rear end and wheel arch panels all required replacement and were quickly removed from the vehicle. Below the fuel tank, one of the fuel tank straps can be seen. These would need to be replaced at a later date due to corrosion.

The front wheel arch panels were in much better condition, but after twenty-one years' service, were past their best. If you look closely around the engine oil access door, sections of green paint can be seen. These would date from her Eastern Scottish/SMT days.

Sister vehicle E190 HSF is pictured on 'death row' at Livingston depot. Although withdrawn due to mechanical problems, she provided a great source of spare seats and interior trim fittings.

By 2002, E187 HSF had lost her front fog lamps. As part of the restoration I removed the metal plates that had been fitted where the fog lamps should be, and was pleasantly surprised to find the fog lamps still in place.

What was even better was that, after a little trial and error with the wiring, the resident electrician at Beith was able to get them working again.

Once the fog lamps were working again, a few fibreglass repairs were required to the bumper area around the fog lamps.

The bottom half of the emergency door required extensive repairs, as did the fuel filler flap.

Above: The slow painstaking task of removing the First Group pink vinyl film is well underway when this photograph was taken. On the areas where it has been removed, the various colours from previous livery schemes can be clearly seen.

Left: By the time this photograph was taken in February 2009, she has been stripped, repaired, sanded and prepared for painting. The extent of the repairs required to the front fibreglass areas can be seen in this photograph.

The next stage in the restoration process was fitting the new aluminium body panels. New panels above the wheel arches have been fitted and new aluminium sheets can be seen, ready to be cut to shape.

When this photograph of E187 HSF was taken on 19 February 2009, all replacement body panels have been fitted and the vehicle has been sanded and prepared for painting.

A few days later and painting has commenced. The window rubbers have been masked off and grey undercoat has started to be applied.

After the undercoat was applied, the light green wedge shapes were painted along with the lower areas of cream, which was officially known as 'off-white'.

Just six days after the last photograph was taken, E187 HSF in nearing completion. The rest of the cream paint has now been applied and the dark green areas have also now been painted.

When I first purchased E187 HSF she was fitted with a three-speed Voith D851.2 gearbox. This was later changed for a four-speed Voith D854.2 gearbox. The replacement four-speed box is pictured awaiting fitting.

Above: When changing the two Voith gearboxes over, it was found that the new four-speed gearbox was slightly longer. This meant that a shorter propshaft had to be manufactured. In this photograph the propshaft has been removed and the original three-speed gearbox is being prepared to also be removed.

Left: During the time I have owned E187 HSF, two of her air suspension bags have been replaced. In this photograph taken in 2015, a new top plate has been welded into place, and a new air suspension bag has also been fitted.

Shortly after purchasing E187 HSF, I decided to purchase a spare Volvo TDH 100 engine and Voith gearbox from a local vehicle dismantler. The replacement engine is pictured awaiting collection, and the Voith gearbox can be seen on the left. The rusty part above the engine is the engine manifold and turbo, and above that the fuel pump can be seen.

On 29 March 2009, the restoration of E187 HSF was complete. She is pictured outside the Beith Transport Museum, getting ready for a short test run.

Left: The cab area has also been restored complete with Wayfarer ticket machine and Eastern Scottish-style cab door.

Below: The majority of the lower-deck seats were replaced with good-quality replacement seats acquired from a similar vehicle that had been withdrawn from service.

Preservation Life: After Restoration the Work Continues

Of the four preserved vehicle's I own, it is safe to say that E187 HSF has required the most ongoing work. After a few years based at the Beith Transport Museum, E187 HSF moved to SVBM (Scottish Vintage Bus Museum) at Lathalmond. She can be regularly found at the GVVT in place of one of my other vehicle as I find it easier to work on vehicles at Glasgow. Over the past few years she has required a fair amount of work to the underside of the vehicle. This has included the fabrication and replacement of most of the wheel arches, which had corroded beyond repair, and the replacement of a number of fuel tank straps. Welding work has also needed to be carried out on certain sections of the chassis, and following this I have painted the chassis with anti-corrosive paint to try and prevent further deterioration of the chassis. New batteries have been fitted and wiring repairs were carried out to the alternator and brake light switch. Both front brake drums have been replaced as they had distorted and damaged the front brake linings, which were also then changed. The front fan assembly had to be replaced with a locally manufactured replacement pulley system. Shortly after I purchased E187 HSF, I noticed the steering did not always work as it should. This was traced to a faulty power steering pump and steering box. Both were changed with acquired parts and this solved the problem. The turbo was replaced while replacing a blown exhaust pipe, and later two of her air suspension bags were changed while replacing the top plates and pistons, which again were heavily corroded.

I was able to source a four-speed Voith gearbox and this was fitted in place of the three-speed Voith gearbox she had inherited at some point during her working life. Changing the gearbox gave a welcome increase in speed and also helped reduce overall fuel consumption. Other more minor repairs have included a replacement thermostat being fitted, which now means the saloon heating works, and also various electrical repairs to interior wiring and to the alternator and battery supply. At times I feel that I must be getting to the stage where everything on the vehicle has been fixed or replaced.

Throughout the years I have owned E187 HSF, despite the work required to keep her on the road, I am still extremely proud of how she looks and have enjoyed getting much use out of her. She has attended a number of open days and events, including an open day in June 2013 at the First Group corporate head office in Aberdeen, where she ended up spending a week. She also took part in filming work in June 2012 for a German film called *Ein Sommer in Schottland* and spent a number of days at various locations in Fife.

The Volvo Citybus was very similar to the Leyland Lion. Eastern Scottish ordered both types of vehicle and examples of both have been preserved. E187 HSF is pictured next to Alexander-bodied Leyland Lion C177 VSF. The bodywork fitted to both vehicles was also very similar, the main difference being the front grill.

In 2011, First Group painted one of their current vehicles, LT52 WUG, into Eastern Scottish livery. The vehicle, a former London Volvo B7 vehicle fitted with Plaxton President bodywork, is pictured next to E187 HSF at SVBM (Scottish Vintage Bus Museum), Lathalmond, during an open day event.

In June 2012, E187 HSF took part in filming work for a German film titled *Ein Sommer in Schottland*. She is pictured near Montrose with the film crew setting up their equipment in the background.

During the filming work E187 HSF spent a number of days based at the Stagecoach Arbroath depot. She is pictured on 11 June 2012 departing Arbroath depot, heading back to SVBM (Scottish Vintage Bus Museum), Lathalmond, following completion of filming.

In June 2013, E187 HSF made the long journey north to Aberdeen to take part in First Group's Aberdeen depot open day. She spent a week based at King Street depot, Aberdeen, and is pictured resting alongside other members of the First Group preserved fleet.

A final photograph on E187 HSF taken in October 2016 outside Glasgow Buchanan bus station. During her time based at Livingston depot in 1994/95, she would often have worked services through to Glasgow Buchanan bus station.

B509 YAT: Plaxton Paramount 3200 Mk 2 Bedford YNT

Vehicle registration number B509 YAT is a Plaxton Paramount 3200-bodied Bedford YNT, which was delivered to France's Coaches, Market Weighton, Yorkshire, in May 1985. She passed to a number of coach operators in England, including Mitcham Belle, before moving north to a Shetland operator in August 1994. In December 1999 she moved to Orkney, where she would see service with a number of operators until she was withdrawn from service in February 2009. B509 YAT was then sold to vehicle dismantler J. Dunsmore, Larkhall, for disposal and was purchased from J. Dunsmore for preservation by the author in November 2009.

Technical Details

Chassis: Bedford YNT
Engine: Bedford Blue Series 500 Turbo, 8.20 Litre
Bodywork: Plaxton Paramount 3200 Mk 2
Seating Capacity: Fifty-Three Coach Seats

Number: ET106889
Gearbox: ZF Six-Speed Manual
Number: 8511NTP2C017
Date First Registered: 1 May 1985

History

Bedford was part of Vauxhall Motors and was therefore part of the General Motors group. They produced commercial vehicles from 1930 until 1987. Being part of Vauxhall they used the Vauxhall Griffin logo. The Bedford Y series of bus and coach chassis were produced between 1970 and 1986, after which Bedford ceased the production of buses and trucks. The Y series chassis was known as a 'lightweight' chassis and the first Y series vehicle was the 10-metre YRQ, which was introduced in 1970. Following this an 11-metre vehicle known as the YRT was introduced in 1972. Both chassis received more powerful engines in 1975 and became known as the YLQ (10 metre) and YMT (11 metre). In 1980 the chassis both received a further upgrade, this time being fitted with a turbocharged engine. The YMT became the YNT and the YLQ became the YMQ/YMP. The final variation of the Y series was introduced in 1984 and was known as the YNV, which featured air suspension. B509 YAT is a Bedford YNT and is therefore an 11-metre vehicle fitted with a turbocharged 8.2-litre engine and six-speed manual ZF gearbox.

The Plaxton Paramount coach was introduced in 1982 and remained in production until 1992. In 1980 the Road Traffic Act of 1930 was changed, which effectively deregulated all long-distance coach services. This resulted in a dramatic increase in coach services, and with many coach operators purchasing coaches from overseas, Plaxton realised they needed a new range of vehicles to win orders. The Paramount vehicle replaced the Supreme model and was radically different, featuring striking 1980s styling. The Paramount was a steel-framed vehicle, and unlike earlier coaches featured a single zintec-coated steel stretch panel in place of the aluminium side panels previously used. This was intended to give a smoother, sleek finish with fewer bodyside mountings. At first the Paramount was offered in a single-deck format at two different heights. The Paramount

3200, as fitted to B509 YAT, was 3.2 meters in height, and the Paramount 3500, the high-floor model, was 3.5 meters tall. Later, in 1984, the Paramount 4000 was introduced. Initially built on Neoplan underframes, the Paramount 4000 was a double-deck coach that was 4 meters in height and featured a lower-deck saloon either at the very rear of the vehicle or directly behind the driver.

One of the most eye-catching parts of the Paramount design was the small feature window fitted just behind the front axle. This remained part of the Paramount design on Mk 1 and Mk 2 vehicles, but was changed on the Mk 3 design. Over the years of production, the majority of the Paramount vehicles constructed were to the 3.2-metre height.

Early Paramount bodies were fitted to Volvo, Leyland and Bedford chassis, but Dennis, Scania and Ford could also be specified. The Mk 2 facelifted Paramount was introduced in 1985, as fitted to B509 YAT, although externally there were relatively few changes compared to the Mk 1 design. Inside, the Mk 2 design featured fabric-covered panels rather than the Formica wood-effect panels seen in the Mk 1 design and a revised entrance design. In 1986 the Paramount was revised again, becoming the Mk 3 design. Externally the design was very different, the most noticeable change being the removal of the sloping side windows and the small feature window, which was replaced with a small pentagonal window behind the entrance door.

B509 YAT was delivered to France's Coaches of Market Weighton, Yorkshire, in May 1985. She was delivered in a two-tone green livery with a red stripe. The livery was applied in one of the standard Paramount livery design schemes offered by Plaxton at the time. She remained with France's Coaches until around February 1993, when it is recorded that she passed to Wright of Worthing. After a year she then passed to Wimco in Mitcham, better known as Mitcham Belle. After a short period of time with Mitcham Belle, B509 YAT moved north of the border to Shalder Coaches of Scalloway, Shetland.

During her time with Shalder Coaches she received the very smart Shalder Coaches black and white livery complete with Puffin logo. Over time Shalder Coaches sold out to Orkney Coaches, with B509 YAT passing to Orkney Coaches. In 1999 Orkney Coaches became part of the Rapson's Group and B509 YAT carried fleet number 451. Later, B509 YAT would receive the standard Rapson's blue livery complete with Orkney logos. During her time on Orkney, 451 was unfortunately involved in a serious road traffic accident. This resulted in major front-end damage and she required an extensive rebuild forward of the front axle. While the repairs were carried out to the vehicle, the steel stretched body panels were replaced with shorter aluminium panels. However, aluminium cannot be stretched in the same way as steel can, and if fitted to vehicles in long lengths the panels can ripple and distort in hot weather. It was for this reason that shorter aluminium panels were fitted, which required extra beading strips to be fitted, covering the joins in the aluminium panels.

In May 2008 Rapson's Group was purchased by Stagecoach Group. At this time B509 YAT passed to the new company and was renumbered from 451 to 59751 in the Stagecoach national fleet numbering system. During her time with Stagecoach she remained allocated to Orkney but was eventually withdrawn from service in February 2009 after almost twenty-four years' service.

B509 YAT was then sold with a number of similar Plaxton Paramount Bedford vehicles to the well-known J. Dunsmore vehicle dismantlers of Larkhall. The vehicles travelled under their own power to Larkhall, leaving Orkney by ferry via St Margaret's Hope.

Operational Service Photographs

Over the years that I have owned B509 YAT I have managed to track down a few photographs of her operating in passenger service, although sadly these don't cover many of the chapters of her working life.

Two members of the France's Coaches fleet are pictured at Scarborough. B509 YAT can be pictured on the left of the photograph and is wearing a smart version of the France's Coaches livery. Her bodywork was constructed by Plaxton, who were located within Scarborough. (Richard Simons)

B509 YAT is pictured at the Ring of Brodgar, Orkney, in 1998 during her time with Shalder Coaches. The Ring of Brodgar is a Neolithic henge and stone circle located near Stromness on the mainland of Orkney. (Alan Robinson)

Two Plaxton-bodied Bedford YNT vehicles rest at Shalder Coaches depot. B509 YAT has Plaxton Paramount Mk 2 bodywork, while PDZ 7762 has the later Mk 3 version of the Plaxton Paramount bodywork. (Campbell Sayers)

By the time this photograph of B509 YAT was taken in 2000 at Stromness, Shalder Coaches had been purchased by Orkney Coaches. Although still retaining her smart Shalder Coaches livery, B509 YAT now carries Rapson Group fleet numbers and a large Orkney fleet name on the windscreen. (Iain MacGregor)

This last photograph of B509 YAT during her time on Orkney was taken at St Margaret's Hope, Orkney, on 26 February 2009. She awaits the ferry to the mainline with a similar Plaxton Paramount vehicle, both of which were ultimately destined for onward transport to J. Dunsmore, vehicle dismantlers, Larkhall. (Chris Platt)

B509 YAT Saved from the Scrapyard – Literally!

Of the four vintage vehicles I now own, the story behind my acquisition of B509 YAT is probably the most interesting.

In October 2009 I was fortunate enough to obtain a four-speed Voith gearbox for my Volvo Citybus E187 HSF to replace the three-speed box she had been fitted with during her time with First. The four-speed gearbox was longer in size, and I therefore required a shorter propshaft to use with the new four-speed box. Rather than shorten the propshaft fitted to the vehicle, I felt it would be better to keep it in case I wished to reinstate the three-speed box at a later date. I therefore decided to purchase a spare propshaft from a local bus dismantler's yard to use instead, which was also from a vehicle fitted with a three-speed box, so the replacement shaft still required shortening.

Since I now owned three preserved buses, I quickly learned to always call into local bus dismantler's yards anytime I was in the area to see if any vehicles being broken up would provide spare parts. Usually when visiting I would, with permission, take photographs of any vehicles awaiting breaking, knowing these could be the last photographs of the vehicle.

On one particular trip to J. Dunsmore's, Larkhall, in October 2009 to purchase the propshaft I required, I noticed a number of Plaxton Paramount coaches in Rapson's livery parked in the far corner of the yard. Some of the coaches were in relatively poor condition, with corrosion clearly setting in. However, one coach, registration B509 YAT, stood out as it looked in remarkably good condition both inside and out. While completing the purchase of the propshaft with the owner of the yard, I made comment about the coaches I had seen in the corner and how one of them looked to be in great condition – far too good for scrap. The owner agreed, adding that the coaches had all been driven down under their own power upon arrival on the ferry from Orkney. The owner agreed with me that it would be a pity if B509 YAT was broken for scrap since she was of a good age and still in good condition.

At first, the yard owner kindly offered the vehicle free to the local museum that I was a member of. However, as spaces available for preserved vehicles were becoming scarce, and since B509 YAT did not fit into the Trust's collection policy, or have an owner to look after her, the offer of the vehicle was politely declined.

I had always liked the Plaxton Paramount design. The radical 1980s styling appealed to me, but also being a steel-framed vehicle with steel panels, a Paramount in good condition was getting hard to find. I liked the idea of owning a coach since that would permit me to visit events further away with ease. Although a Bedford would not have been my first choice for a coach, I quickly realised this might be my only chance of owning a Plaxton Paramount vehicle. Therefore, without even driving the vehicle, I made the yard owner an offer for the vehicle, which was quickly accepted. The vehicle was paid for that afternoon, and once we had prepared her for the short journey back to the museum in Glasgow, B509 YAT departed from J. Dunsmore's yard later that evening, literally having been saved from the scrapyard. Now what would have happened to her if I hadn't called in for a propshaft that day!

She was initially housed in the GVVT premises at Bridgeton, Glasgow, alongside my two Clydeside vehicles, GCS 50V and HSD 73V, while I arranged alternative storage for her. After a few weeks I was delighted to learn that she had been accepted to join my Volvo Citybus E187 HSF at SVBM (Scottish Vintage Bus Museum), Lathalmond.

B509 YAT is pictured in October 2009, awaiting her fate at J. Dunsmore, vehicle dismantlers, Larkhall. This photograph was taken on the day I inspected B509 YAT and discussed with the yard owner the prospect of her being saved for preservation.

Despite being twenty-four years old when this photograph was taken, her interior was found to be in excellent condition. The moquette used for the seats was a little on the bright side.

A late evening photograph taken on 27 November 2009 shows B509 YAT leaving J. Dunsmore's yard at Larkhall, saved and ready for her new preserved life.

B509 YAT is pictured the following day at GVVT. I was now able to have a good look over her and found her to be in good overall condition.

An added bonus was the discovery of some spare parts that had been placed into the boot of the coach.

Restoration

As mentioned, with B509 YAT awaiting her fate in a breaker's yard, I was not able to get a good look over her or take her for a run before deciding to purchase her. I had to go with my gut feeling and felt that if she had been so well looked after inside and out, hopefully she would have been in good running order too.

As part of my offer to purchase her, the owner of the dismantler's yard had given me permission to return and remove interior fittings and items of body trim from the other vehicles in the yard. This proved invaluable and a great number of items were acquired. When I got back to the museum with the spare parts I had acquired, I got a pleasant surprise when I opened the boot of B509 YAT: her previous owner in Orkney had kindly put all his spare parts inside. This included two radiators, hubs, brake shoes and an air tank – all good and valuable spares. The first issue to be resolved with B509 YAT was to get her back on the DVLA system. By the time I had acquired her, she had inadvertently been recorded as scrapped. I contacted the DVLA to explain what had happened to the vehicle and provided them with date-stamped photographs to prove her existence. A new V5 vehicle logbook arrived soon after, which enabled me to submit the vehicle for an MOT test and to finally tax her. She moved shortly afterwards to SVBM (Scottish Vintage Bus Museum), Lathalmond, in March 2010.

Like many of the other vehicles I have purchased, B509 YAT was in good overall condition. As she had now passed her MOT test and was taxed, I decided to get some use from the vehicle before beginning her restoration. She attended some local events, and in May 2010 provided our transport for a weekend trip to Blackpool.

Her three-month restoration began in January 2011 and was carried out at the GVVT museum. The coachbuilder that had carried out the earlier work on my Leyland Leopard GCS 50V carried out the majority of this work as well. He began with a survey of the bodywork, and between us we decided which panels should be replaced and which panels could be repaired. As mentioned earlier, this Paramount was a bit different in that her long stretched-steel body panels had been replaced with shorter replacement aluminium panels. Overall, most of the panels were in good condition; only a few needed changing and most were able to be repaired. A lot of the body trim and mouldings were either badly damaged or missing. This could have occurred when the coach was being re-panelled earlier in her working life. Much of the trim was able to be replaced with the spares I had acquired or purchased direct from Plaxton.

Once the body trim was replaced, attention turned to the rear of the vehicle. One of the iconic features of the Paramount design is the rear illuminated panel above the boot lid. This would often be used to advertise the owning company details, with slogans like 'Luxury Travel' added. Over the years B509 YAT had lost her illuminated panel and the glass had been replaced with an aluminium panel. I had managed to acquire a replacement glass panel from a similar vehicle being broken for scrap. The wiring for the illuminated panel was reinstated before the replacement glass panel was repainted and refitted. The metal panels at the rear of the vehicle that hold the rear lights in place were found to be badly corroded and these along with the roof-mounted air intake vents were replaced. Work then turned to the front of the vehicle, where repairs were required to the removable front grill and headlamp surrounds. I have never been particularly skilled with spray paint, but a good friend of mine with a steady hand managed to repair and repaint the three silver/grey panels at the front to look as good as new.

Repairs to B509 YAT were progressing well by this stage, although when I saw her with the front panels removed and sanded down ready for painting, I thought she still had a long way to go. Once the bodywork repairs were complete and the vehicle had been prepared for painting, she received a coat of grey undercoat followed by a repaint into Rapson's blue livery. When I first purchased B509 YAT I was not sure what livery I should restore her in. I was tempted to repaint her into a livery long lost from the deregulation period of history – for example the white and silver Clydeside Quicksilver livery that similar vehicles previously carried. In the end I decided to stick with the same Rapson's livery she currently carried. Rapson's became a large operator during the post-deregulation years, and since they had now been acquired by Stagecoach, I felt it was appropriate that a vehicle should be preserved in their livery.

While work continued on the exterior, the vehicle received a full service, and at the same time some of the vehicle's metal brake lines were replaced as they were also found to be corroded. The underside received a clean and was painted, and a troublesome starter motor was rewired and ultimately replaced. The interior of the vehicle was in very good condition for her age and she had clearly been well looked after. She had a full set of matching seats, which over time had been fitted with seatbelts. They were not, however, reclining seats. I learned of a Plaxton Paramount 4000 double-deck coach that had been withdrawn for scrap in a nearby yard. The seats fitted to this coach were the later squarer reclining seats that many Paramount vehicles received. I decided to purchase the lot, including some spare matching fabric and a table. Over the next few weeks I slowly changed the seats over to the new reclining examples, and fitted the table near the back at the nearside. This was not as easy as first thought, since the two different style of seats had two different seat frames and legs. Finally, all the seats were changed over and the roof runner panels were re-covered in the spare fabric to match the rest of the coach. The original seats fitted were sold on for further use and one set of seats in the coach was turned around to provide a set of four seats around the newly fitted table.

Restoration was finally completed on 8 April 2011 and I was delighted to see B509 YAT back on the road, looking extremely smart in her fresh coat of Rapson's blue livery.

The restoration of B509 YAT began in January 2011. When this photograph of B509 YAT was taken in February 2011, she had been sanded, ready for repaint. Replacement body mouldings have also been fitted and the front panel is receiving fibreglass repairs.

One of the iconic features of the Plaxton Paramount design was the large illuminated rear glass panel. Over the years this had been removed from B509 YAT and a painted aluminium panel was inserted instead. This photograph of B509 YAT shows the old metal panel having been removed and the florescent light reinstalled. Repairs are also underway to the rear light fittings.

Left: Much of the bodywork of B509 YAT was still in very good condition; she had clearly been well looked after during her time in Orkney. Some panels did require some minor repairs with filler, however.

Below: Once her bodywork repairs were completed and replacement trim was fitted, B509 YAT received a coat of grey undercoat. She is pictured within the paint bay at GVVT with her windows and body trim masked off, ready for the next coat of paint.

Eight days after the last photograph was taken, B509 YAT has received a coat of the lighter blue paint.

This photograph of B509 YAT was taken on 10 March 2011 in the yard of GVVT, just a few days after the last photograph and just fourteen days after painting had commenced.

Above: The underside of the vehicle was found to be in reasonable condition for its age. Over time the underside of the vehicle has received a clean and has been painted with anti-corrosive paint. The brake lines, which can be clearly seen in this photograph, were also replaced.

Left: Although the seats fitted to B509 YAT were in excellent condition, I decided to change them for a set of reclining Plaxton Paramount seats. I also re-covered the roof running panels in the same fabric to match the new seats.

The replacement seats were fitted to the vehicle over the course of a few weekends. The seats were heavy and awkward to replace, and for the next few months I had many bruises to show for the work undertaken.

The replacement illuminated rear panel was refurbished and repainted prior to refitting. The replacement panel was acquired from a similar vehicle being dismantled at a nearby yard.

The removable front panel also received minor repairs before being repainted and refitted to the vehicle. All painting work on the vehicle was applied by brush rather than spray. A time-served painter carried out the work and provided an excellent finish.

Once the painting was completed, the vehicle was fitted with large Orkney fleet names, applied in the Rapson Group style. Fitting was not easy since the three different colours had to be lined up and applied on top of each other. The thin, light blue line on the livery was actually adhesive tape and ensured a neat, clean finish.

The replacement illuminated rear panel had now been fitted and completed the rear-end restoration. The lighting behind the panel had also been reinstated.

The completed B509 YAT is pictured in the grounds of SVBM in April 2011.

Preservation Life So Far

A Bedford vehicle would never have been my first choice, and I would have much rather purchased a Volvo or Leyland coach. Over the years I have owned B509 YAT, I considered replacing her engine with a Cummins B series or preferably a Cummins C series engine. As yet I have refrained from doing so as I like the fact she has her original type of engine as fitted from new. At times she can be politely described as challenging to drive! She is fine on a flat road or even downhill, but as soon as a hill is encountered the driver is required to work hard and make frequent gear changes. All gears are present and correct, although it is fair to say that they are not all located exactly where you would expect to find them, if indeed you can find them at all. Since her restoration was completed in April 2011, she has, like my other vehicles, attended various open day events, and also undertook a trip for museum members from GVVT to Beamish Museum in County Durham. She also undertook a birthday trip for a friend to Blair Drummond Safari Park, near Stirling. During the visit to Blair Drummond, I was most relieved when we completed the drive through the lion enclosure without breaking down.

She is currently temporarily off the road, awaiting a repair to her clutch system. It is planned for this work to be completed in the early part of 2018, allowing her to return to the road once more. For the future I intend to pay a visit back to Orkney with B509 YAT, possibly to coincide with the annual Orkney Vintage Rally, which is held each August.

B509 YAT is pictured during a weekend trip for a few friends to Blackpool in June 2010. The Blackpool pleasure beach can be seen in the background as B509 YAT gets ready to head back north.

In October 2011, B509 YAT undertook a day trip to the Beamish Museum, County Durham, for GVVT members.

B509 YAT took a group of friends to Blair Drummond Safari Park on 21 April 2012. She is pictured with one of the park's friendlier residents upon arrival.

While her passengers enjoyed a pleasant afternoon at the safari park, B509 YAT basks in the April sunshine. I was most relieved once the coach had made it safely through the lion enclosure during our visit.